Moving Out of Dream Castles

Where Dreams Become Reality

by
Tjuana "Ladawn" Callahan-Stewart

Copyright © 2007 Tjuana "Ladawn" Callahan-Stewart

All rights reserved. No part of this book may be reproduced in any form or by any means, electronic or mechanical, including photo-copying, recording, or by any information storage and retrieval system, without written permission from the author. This excludes a reviewer who may quote brief passages in a review. For additional information, please contact the author at ladawn_3@yahoo.com.

Published by G Publishing, LLC

Cover Design: SOS Graphics and Designs
Editor: Francene Ambrose-Gunn

ISBN 13: 978-0-9790691-7-8
       10: 0-9790691-7-3

Library of Congress Control Number: 2007902484

Published and printed in the United States of America

www.poetrybyladawn.com

Table of Contents

The Word – Ephesians 5:1-20	7
Introduction	9
Chapter 1 – Dream Castles	11
Day Dreaming	12
Dream Castles	13
Hopeless Romantic	16
Intense Observation	18
The Great Deception	21
Blind Love	23
Cheater?	25
Adam and Eve	26
Pouring My Heart Out	28
Chapter 2 – Transformation	31
Destiny	32
All My Fault	33
Just Tell the Truth	36
Eyes Wide Open	38
No Regrets	41
Not My Own	43
No Sex Before the Wedding	44
Love Blossoms	46
A Bottle for Tears	48
The Drama	49
Friends and Users	51
Patience	53
Turtle Gear	55
Am I Ready?	56

Chapter 3 – Manifestation	*59*
God's Definition of Love	60
Desires of the Heart	61
Reaching the Impossible	63
Subliminal Messages	64
Just a Lookin'	66
Know This	68
Unevenly Yoked	70
Understanding	71
Voices From the Soul	72
Gentle Tiger	74
Hidden Treasures	76
First Kiss	78
Chapter 4 – Appreciation	*79*
Forgetting the Past	80
Lifetime Friend	82
R-E-S-P-E-C-T	83
Hello Sunshine	85
No Turning Back	88
Romance Without Sex	89
Desires	90
Behind the Scenes	91
Counting My Blessing	94
Intimate Friends	96
Bubbles	98
Fortune Cookies	99
Mesmerized	100

Chapter 5 – Reflections   *100*

Absence Makes the Heart Grow Fonder   101
Gratitude   103
Marriage Bed Undefiled   105

The Word-Ephesians 5:1-20 (NLT)

Imitate God, therefore, in everything you do, because you are his dear children. Live a life filled with love, following the example of Christ. He loved us and offered himself as a sacrifice for us, a pleasing aroma to God.

Let there be no sexual immorality, impurity, or greed among you. Such sins have no place among God's people. Obscene stories, foolish talk, and coarse jokes - these are not for you. Instead, let there be thankfulness to God. You can be sure that no immoral, impure, or greedy person will inherit the Kingdom of Christ and of God. For a greedy person is an idolater, worshiping the things of this world.

Don't be fooled by those who try to excuse these sins, for the anger of God will fall on all who disobey him. Don't participate in the things these people do. For once you were full of darkness, but now you have light from the Lord. So live as people of light! For this light within you produces only what is good and right and true.

Carefully determine what pleases the Lord. Take no part in the worthless deeds of evil and darkness; instead, expose them. It is shameful even to talk about the things that ungodly people do in secret. But their evil intentions will be exposed when the light shines on them, for the light makes everything visible. This is why it is said,

> "Awake, O sleeper,
> rise up from the dead,
> and Christ will give you light."

So be careful how you live. Don't live like fools, but like those who are wise. Make the most of every opportunity in these evil days. Don't act thoughtlessly, but understand what the Lord wants you to do. Don't be drunk with wine, because that will ruin your life. Instead, be filled with the Holy Spirit, singing psalms and hymns and spiritual songs among yourselves, and making music to the Lord in your hearts. And give thanks for everything to God the Father in the name of our Lord Jesus Christ.

Introduction

I used to think that I was the only one living in a Dream Castle, but now I am sure that is not true. So, I decided to share my thoughts. I pray this book reaches the hearts and minds of those who can identify with these words.

I was a young woman with a vivid imagination, always thinking about the man of my dreams. I was so preoccupied with dreaming that I did not know the difference between dreams and reality. There was a list of qualities and characteristics this man of my dreams displayed and I expected every man I dated to possess those qualities. When they didn't, I was crushed, disillusioned, depressed and dismayed. My reality was a dream that I expected each of them to live up to.

Even though I was headed for self destruction, I continued this way for years. I began each relationship believing that I had met the man of my dreams. It's sad that I was so naïve and trusting of men I didn't take the time to know. I attached the qualities of Mr. Right to him and trusted him to be that way. It was unrealistic to expect every man to be Mr. Right, especially since they had no idea who this dream man was.

After years of depression and low self-esteem, I stopped. I realized that I had not been successful in finding Mr. Right at all, and I was living in a Dream Castle. So I took some time out for self-examination and Jesus met me there. He spent many days and nights in the Dream Castle with me unveiling the truth about me, my relationships, and my sin. Then, He moved me out of the Dream Castle into the Mansion of His Love. After resting there a while, I was equipped with the truth and power which enabled me to develop fulfilling and realistic relationships.

This book is actually a journal of my thoughts as I went through this process of change. It is a collection of poems, letters, essays and prayers with a central plot. As you read, I hope that you experience the change. I am praying that these words will encourage you to move out of your Dream Castle also.

So I invite you to sit down, read, reflect and pray.

Chapter One

Dream Castles

The heart is deceitful above all things, and desperately wicked: who can know it?
Jeremiah 17:9 (KJV)

Day Dreaming

Thoughts of you bring a smile to my face.
Memories of you are full of delight.
Dreams of you produce anxious anticipation.
In my mind are vivid images of tomorrow
enticing me with visions of the dawn.

Dream Castles

I can see it my mind.
So beautiful . . .
I'm always building
ideas in my head.
Visions of perfection
Perfect in my sight
So vivid
So real
Every detail in place
Every color and design
Every shape and texture
Every segment and frame
I view in the theatre
of my mind.

Dream Castles

Moving Out of Dream Castles

I can hear it in my ears.
What he'll say to me
and how he'll say it.
Lovely words
Just what I wanted to hear
All the right questions
All the right answers
A perfect melody
So sharp
So clear
It sings to me
Every sound and pitch
Every rhythm and pace
The tone and grace
of his voice
I record in the songs
of my mind.

I can feel it in my heart
and my soul gets happy
for what my eyes and ears
have created.
It must be real –
what I see and hear
becomes a part of me.

Chapter 1 - Dream Castles

As I feel what I feel
I know what I know
A perfect expression
So confident
So sincere
It touches me
The heart and the passion
Every pleasure and pain
Every caress and embrace
holds me in the chambers
of my mind.

I can smell it and taste it.
Mmm – so good
More than my senses can stand
Gotta have it right now
Just gotta have it
A day to remember
So delicious
So sweet
It entices me.
The aroma and flavor
Every palate and fragrance
The essence and desire
thrills me in the senses
of my mind.

The test lies in deciding
if this is real or
am I only dreaming.

Dream Castles

Hopeless Romantic

It's true
I don't love you
I don't think
I ever did
I just loved
the idea of romance.
I hate to admit it.
Never took the time
to know you.
Only longing
for the feelings
that you give.

Sad, sad affair
to leave you
standing there
with nothing but time
and false intentions.
Selfish inhibitions
and shallow intuitions
leave me lonely
with no one
to call my own.

Chapter 1 - Dream Castles

Love –
I do now know.
Never took
the time to show
the true person
who's living inside of me.
Dare I not decide
to gaze into your mind
and see the precious
treasures that are there.

I pray you can forgive me
and we can start again.
I'd like to take
the time to be your friend.
I'm sick and tired of hiding.
I'm lonely and afraid.
I'd like to know what
loving really is.

Intense Observation

You're just curious . . .
Aren't you?
Wondering what it'd
be like
being with me.

You don't believe
what your eyes
are seeing.
You can't understand
what your heart
is feeling.
Enchanted by
what your ears
are hearing
still you can't
figure me out.

Could I really be
who I appear to be.
or am I just
a mirage
to a thirsty man
wandering the desert
too long.

Chapter 1 - Dream Castles

You never thought
you'd meet me.
Did you?
Gave up long time ago.
Meeting me in this
space and time
seems like a low blow.

A strong man
wonders why
give up someone
after waiting
so long.

You want to
come closer
but you can't.
Wishing for
a touch
but you won't.
With great will
and determination
you struggle
with uncertain knowing.

Moving Out of Dream Castles

Staring closely
from a distance,
turn and walk away.
I could never truly be
what you'd want from me.
Forgive me for inviting you.
With humility I bow . . .
Married men
must remember
their sacred wedding vow.

Chapter 1 - Dream Castles

The Great Deception

One day I woke up
and realized
I was only deceiving myself.
I said I would never
do that again
when deep down inside
I planned it.
Scheming and dreaming
in my mind
Allowing my flesh
to take control
I lied to myself
believing the lie
damaging my own soul.

Don't ever deny your desires
Believing they'll just go away.
Be true to yourself
and your Heavenly Father.
He will show you the way.
Desires are stronger
than you alone.
You can't handle them
on your own.
Talk to the Father
He has the power
to help you
up out of that hole.

Moving Out of Dream Castles

One day I looked up
and realized,
they only did
what I allowed.
Looking for love
in all the wrong places.
My head was
up in a cloud.

Never really
loving myself
I expected them
to receive me,
cover the pain
in my soul
and fill this
empty being.

Look to Jesus
for your healing.
He can quench
that thirsty feeling.
Invite Him
into your soul
and let Him
have control.
He will wash
the guilty stain
and make you
whole again.

Blind Love

Day dreaming again -
I close my eyes,
and see what
I want to see.
Believing the lies,
faking the truth,
although it's
a fallacy.

I cover the pain
and look over
the shame
not wanting
to face the game.
I don't believe
a word they say.
My lover would
never do me
that way.
It's all a lie.
They don't know.
Without him
I would
surely die.

Moving Out of Dream Castles

My hope is in him.
Can't start over again.
One day he'll change.
'Til then I'll pretend.
It'll be all right
if I hang on tight
close my eyes
and keep my
dream in sight.

Chapter 1 - Dream Castles

Cheater?

You gotta lotta nerve
You gotta lotta balls
Calling him a cheater
an' you ain't even hitched.

He's free as a bird
and wild as a cat
'til he walks the aisle
and signs a contract.

He ain't made no promise
to be with you only
An' you makin' wedding plans.
He ain't even asked an'
you ain't hearin' what he's sayin'.

I know you been talkin'.
You wanna get hitched.
But, that load he just
ain't ready to carry.

You just won't listen.
You won't admit.
He loves you dearly
but he don't wanna commit.

Be for real.
Hold your tongue.
Make your decision
and move on.

Adam and Eve

After breathing life into man
God gave him purpose.
The words He spoke to Adam
gave him meaning.
Alone in the garden
he got instructions.
When Adam accepted
these words
God gave him Eve.

A simple lesson learned --
Let's stay in order.
Before seeking out a mate
let's seek the Lord.
Never really satisfied
you'll wander till you die
without knowing the
real blessing in your being.

Ladies here's a tip.
Be realistic.
Take a closer look.
Does he have meaning?
Has he been alone with God?
Has he listened for instruction?
Or is he wandering
around without direction?

Chapter 1 - Dream Castles

God created Eve
to be a helper.
If he doesn't have a goal,
How can you help him?
Wander with him if you will.
You'll be wandering until
he decides to get with God
and find his purpose.

A wandering man
is not committed.
He goes from place to place
without contentment.
Let him wander on.
He'll wander till he dies
or finds the destination
in his journey.

Pouring My Heart Out

Lord,

I know I've been overlooking you. I've been treating you like an outsider - like a co-worker that I only call on when church ministry needs to be done. I haven't acknowledged you as a friend I share all of my thoughts with. Teach me what it means to thirst for you – to crave you – to open my pores and allow your love to flow in.

Thank you for being so merciful – so gracious – and so kind. When I'm alone and want so badly to talk to someone help me to turn within and pour my heart out to you. I need you. Help me to walk in the true meaning of making you a friend that sticks closer than a brother. I want to be able to share with you my every wish and desire – my smallest thought to my greatest dream. I want to know how to rely on your guidance to do the things that you would have me to do.

Give me a concrete assurance that you are not in some distant place visiting me from time to time. You're not living in some house across town. You're not up there somewhere in the sky. You're not a person I can leave at home while I commute around the city from place to place.

Chapter 1 - Dream Castles

Your spirit lives within me. Everywhere I go you are there. You are a caring, wise, loving companion. You want to be here helping me in every situation no matter how trivial. As I grow, I want to be eager for your communion and zealous for your touch.

Chapter Two

Transformation

The wisdom of the prudent is to
understand his way:
But the folly of fools is deceit.
Proverbs 14:8 (KJV)

Destiny

Lord,

What do you have in my destiny?
Lead me, guide and direct me
into my destiny. Lead me away from
anything that will steer me off of
the path you have already prepared
for me.

I'm trusting you.

Chapter 2 - Transformation

All My Fault

That man!
All his fault!
That's what I used to say.
I was perfect
and he was not.

That man!
All his fault!
He did it to me.
I didn't know
he had a plot.

He ruined my life.
He messed with my head.
He stole my money.
He got in my bed.
That's what I used to say
in former days.

It was all his fault
so I thought and believed.
He had some kind of
trick up his sleeve.
I didn't expect
him to love me
and leave.

Moving Out of Dream Castles

I know better now.
Looking back I see
that all the blame
belongs to me.
I walked around
with eyes wide shut.
I thought wisdom
and knowledge
was an insult.

I did it my way
not looking at all
to the handwriting written
all over the wall.
And listen – Oh no.
You couldn't tell me a thing.
I knew this would lead
to me getting my ring.

Looking at those dream castles
In my head – They became reality.
I didn't wake up.
I stayed there sleeping
while life came by and
decided for me
how I would live
and what I would be.

Chapter 2 - Transformation

It's not his fault
Didn't stick to my guns.
Lowered my standards
and shifted my funds.
It's not his fault
I decided to be
exactly what
he wanted from me
instead of being myself.
Setting my goals
Living my life
Remembering my soul
Doing what's right
It was all my fault
I admit and take
full responsibility.

Just Tell the Truth

Don't lie to me
Don't steal from me
and Don't stand me up
These make a foundation
for good communication.

Just tell the truth
instead of lies.
No matter what
I may decide.
Tell the truth
when it hurts.
Truth may sting
but lies divide.
Please don't take
without permission.
It puts me in
a bad position.
Watching every
move you make
and hiding things
for safety's sake.

Chapter 2 - Transformation

Don't make me wait.
There's no debate.
Let me know
you're running late.
If you decide to
change you mind
calling me
would be no crime.
Tell the truth
Don't feed me lines.
No deceit
of any kind.
My intellect
needs your respect.
Give me the truth
and nothing less.

Eyes Wide Open

Keep your eyes open
so you can see clearly
the good and bad in a person
and even the ugly.
Ask lots of questions.
Watch what they do
and you will be able
to tell what is true.
Patiently withstand
the test of time.
Only gamblers move
on the drop of a dime.

Experience teaches
lessons are learned
as character builds
respect is earned.
Share many moments.
Add up the cost.
Know what you have
before it is lost.
Measure the hours.
Honor the days.
Treasure the months
in so many ways.

Chapter 2 - Transformation

Say what you mean.
Mean what you do.
Loyalty is priceless
and patience a virtue.
Stick together
in sunshine and rain.
True friends share
in joy and pain.
Laugh out loud.
Cry without shame.
Speak your mind
and forget the game.

Face the problems.
Don't push them aside.
Don't hide them behind
the fear and pride.

Settle issues –
great and small.
Together we stand.
Divided we fall.
Don't hold on to
good intentions.
Follow your
insight and intuition.

Moving Out of Dream Castles

Pray for each other.
Ask God to reveal
what is fictitious
and what is real.
Carefully listen
Don't ignore
signs along the road
and wisdom at the door.
Uphold God's standard.
Don't settle for less.
He's waiting to give you
no less than the best.

Chapter 2 - Transformation

No Regrets

As much as possible live life without regrets
Don't lend what you're not willing to give.
Don't risk what you're not willing to lose.
Don't cosign loans you can't pay alone.
Don't make long term commitments with
short-term friends.
Agree on principles and set limitations.
Know how to deal with subtle temptations.

Getting high and losing control
is never the way to go.
Abstaining from sex before the wedding
helps to keep your thinking clear.
Don't place yourself in temptation
you know you can't resist.
Ask the Holy Spirit's guidance
every single day.
Search for Godly wisdom
to help you along the way.
When you feel frustration
seek the lesson you must learn
and obey.

Respect yourself
and others will do the same.
Be slow to speak and quick to listen.
Answer an angry tone with a soft voice.
Quickly apologize when you're wrong.
Step forward first even when you're right.
Don't make commitments without
understanding expectations.
Don't expect anything without discussion.

Give expecting nothing in return.
Discuss goals and come to an agreement.
Stick to your word with integrity.
If you change your mind let the other person know.
When others fall short forgive and refocus.
Don't try to cover up your errors.
Remember no one is perfect including yourself.

Chapter 2 - Transformation

Not my Own

We give glory back to God
by using our bodies for his purpose.
Sex outside of marriage is never right.
Our bodies were not made for that.
Our bodies are parts and members of Christ.
Should we take part of Christ
and sinfully join Him to another?

I don't think so.

Consider this.
When a man and woman have sex
they hook up together.
In God's sight, the two become one.
So, if we truly hook up with Christ,
how can you hook up with another in sin?

Run from this temptation.
No other sin affects the body like this one.
We're sinning against our own bodies!
God sent His Holy Spirit to live inside of us.
We don't own these bodies.
We're God's property.

No Sex Before the Wedding

No intercourse
No oral sex
No s-e-x of any kind
No finger sex
No anal sex
Keep your hands
off my behind.

Don't touch my thighs.
Don't feel my breasts
for that would not be wise.
Don't lick my neck.
Don't bite my lobes.
Let's not have
our natures rise.

It will be hard
I must admit
when longings are
filled with emptiness.
God will help
us to withstand
if we sincerely
seek His plan.

Chapter 2 - Transformation

And when the
wedding day arrives
the wedded bliss
will come alive.
But, if wedding vows
we do not take
then friendship
will not ever break.

Love Blossoms

Love God first.
Then look within.
God wants to be
your closest friend.
He loves you –
Why not love yourself?
Stop putting your life
up on a shelf.

Loving yourself means
building your body,
feeding your mind,
and filling your soul.
Loving yourself means
setting your standards
and giving your all
to conquer your goals.
Looking to God
for definition
instead of filling
man-made positions.
God knows you better than
you know yourself.
He will reveal your
treasures of wealth.

Chapter 2 - Transformation

Rays of sunshine
enter your soul
then love blossoms
start to unfold.
Water those blossoms.
Treat them with care.
As they multiply
you will be
able to share.

A Bottle for Tears

God keeps your tears of sorrow
in a special bottle.
He know the meaning
of your moaning.
He reads your tears
as they are flowing
and writes the issues
in the chapter of this year.
When the bottle fills
He takes away your tears
to pour into the chamber of His heart.

When the morrow comes
and broken hearts are mending
God brings another bottle
for tears of joy that's never ending.
The bottle fills again
with joy instead of sorrow
and hope for your tomorrow.

Psalm 56:8 (NLT)
You keep track of all my sorrows.
You have collected all my tears in your bottle.
You have recorded each one in your book.

Chapter 2 - Transformation

The Drama

As a single woman, there are some things I had to eliminate.
Things that used to stress me out,
I don't even have to think about.

Like:

Will he respect me in the morning?
Thinking he just wants my body
Midnight booty calls when I'm tired
Allowing good sex to influence my decisions
Birth control pills
Wondering if he's with another woman tonight
Is that woman trying to steal my man?
Someone asking, "Are you pregnant?"
Oh God, my period is late!
A pregnancy test
Hearing him say, "That's not my baby."
My man requesting a paternity test!
Wondering if he'll pay child support
Wondering how I can take care of a baby
A short pay check and a sick baby
Adding up the cost of Child Care
Adding up the cost of milk and diapers
My own Baby Mama Drama

God gave me a cure for all that stuff.
I'm more peaceful and secure.
Some of you know what I'm talking about
and some of you don't have a clue.
These issues no longer plague my life.
They no longer bring me pain.
He gave me the perfect remedy
by teaching me to abstain.
No, it's not easy.
It took some time to learn by
allowing the Holy Spirit
to give me power and self-control.
All the energy I used to use living in the drama
is occupied by living to serve my Heavenly Father.

Chapter 2 - Transformation

Friends and Users

Friends tell you the truth
when you'd rather hear lies.
Users lie to you
when you'd rather hear the truth.
Friends walk with you
when others walk away.
Users walk away
when you need somebody with you.
Friends disagree with you
when you expect agreement
Users agree with you
cause disagreement isn't pleasing.

Friends come to see you
when you'd rather not be seen.
Users only see you
when you're ready to be seen.
Friends hear complaining
and stop you in your tracks.
Users join in complaining
just to win you over.
Friends bring in hope
when all seems hopeless.
Users see you hopeless
and leave you in despair.

Friends respect your values
even though they don't agree.
Users disregard your values
when they limit pleasures.
Friends give encouragement
that pushes you all the way.
Users bring discouragement
that keeps you in their playpen.
Friends know when to speak
and when it's time to listen.
Users never listen
because they're always talking.

Friends will cry with you
in the midst of your sorrow.
Users use your tears
to hold you down in weakness.
Friends will draw the line
of use and abuse.
Users cross the line
when abusing brings them pleasure.
Friends want to see you grow.
Users want to use you.
Friends are with you throughout life.
Users stay as long as they use you.

Chapter 2 - Transformation

Patience

"Fools rush in."
That's what they say.
Some lose patience any way.

No need to rush.
Take your time.
Get to know what's on his mind.

Discuss purpose and intentions.
Find out if you both agree.
Then watch, wait and see.

Time will tell the story.
Does he walk that walk?
Or just talk that talk?

You need experience
and observation
in many different situations.

Ask the Father to reveal
if your heart he will steal.
Listen to the Holy Spirit.
Forget your selfish intuition.

Moving Out of Dream Castles

Don't decide so quick to marry.
Seek God's advice in earnest praying.
Clearly hear what He is saying.

Decisions we make everyday
affect our every tomorrow.
They bring a life full of joy
or many days of sorrow.

Chapter 2 - Transformation

Turtle Gear

Even though I forgive you, deep down inside I put up my turtle gear. "Never again," I say. I'll continue to be cordial, but letting my guard down again won't happen. My shield is up now. I decided that I could still love you from the inside of my shell.

You're right! I had doubts. Most people apologize just to get out of trouble. People tend to say "I'm sorry" when in bad situations. As soon as they are out of the jam, they go right back to the same old things. They don't have true repentance. They just want out of the uncomfortable zone.

Yes, I'm afraid sometimes. A turtle is a fragile, tender creature inside of the shell. That's why the shell is so hard on the outside. This turtle has taken a few knocks. As long as I can stay inside, the vibration can't really get to the soft spot. Coming out of my shell means I expose you to the soft parts.

I expect you to be very careful. Wounding me while exposed can cause serious damage. I'll just have to believe that God will help you in keeping your promise to love me.

Am I Ready?

Ready to face the truth
Ready to bury the shame
Ready to stop pretending
Ready to let go of the past
Ready to look at myself

Am I ready?

Ready to use my mistakes
as step of progress
Ready to get up, dust myself
and start again
Ready to repent, turn around
and look to Jesus
Ready to forgive myself

Am I ready?

Ready to stop trying to please man
and start trying to please God
Ready to follow God's agenda
instead of following my own
Ready to take time for God
Ready to put God first

Am I ready?

Chapter 2 - Transformation

Ready to release the pain
to be healed
Ready to confess my sins
and be delivered
Ready to let go of pride
and be redeemed
Ready to obey the Truth
and be free

Am I ready?

Ready to enjoy the present
day by day
Ready to look at life
every bit of it
Ready to enhance the good
and correct the ugly
Ready to be myself
come what may

Am I ready?

Ready to see my beauty
and stop hiding
Ready to see my abilities
despite my frustration
Ready to show who I really am
because I accept myself
Ready to share myself
knowing my significance

Am I ready?

Moving Out of Dream Castles

Ready to risk my heart
and give again
Ready to give up life
and live again
Ready to forgive my enemies
and love again
Ready to give up my time
and be a friend

Am I ready?

Ready to tell the truth
with it hurts
Ready to walk the extra mile
when it's needed
Ready to seek out understanding
and mix it in with patience
Ready to share good and bad times
without hesitation

Am I ready?

Chapter Three

Manifestation

**Trust in the Lord with all your heart;
do not depend on your own
understanding.
Seek his will in all you do,
and he will show you which path to take.
Proverbs 3:5-6 (NLT)**

God's Definition of Love

If I had the gift of being able to speak in other languages without learning them and could speak in every language in all of heaven and earth, but didn't love people, I would only be making noise. If I had the gift of prophecy and knew everything about everything, but didn't love, what good would it do? Even if I had the gift of faith so that I could speak to a mountain and make it move, I would still be nothing at all without love. If I gave everything I have to poor people – even if I were burned alive for preaching the Gospel but didn't love others, it would be of no value whatsoever.

Love is very patient and kind. Love is never jealous or envious. It's never boastful or proud. Love is never high minded nor selfish nor rude. Love does not demand its own way. It is neither irritable nor edgy. It does not hold grudges and will hardly even notice when others do it wrong. It is never glad about injustice, but rejoices whenever truth wins out. Love conquers all. Love always believes and always expects the best. Love never fails.

Paraphrased from II Corinthians 13:1-7

Chapter 3 - Manifestation

Desires of the Heart

Why am I so attracted to him Lord, Why?
How can we glorify you together Lord, How?
What is Your purpose for our bonding?
What role am I supposed to play?
I don't want to screw up this opportunity.

Why am I so attracted to him?
Sometimes he consumes my thought,
my dreams and my motives for action.
Please forgive me when my motives are impure.

I want to know what we must accomplish together.
As You look down at the big picture,
how do we compliment or blend in Your
masterpiece?
What is it that pleases You in this bonding?

I love you Lord and I want to please You.
How can we magnify Your name together?
What unique creation do we form
that no other two people can manifest?
How do our colors blend in Your eye?
What masterpiece do You behold?

Why do I love him so much?
I adore even the sound of his voice
and the glance of his eyes.
His words are gentle and sweet to my ears.
I feel a warm, loving person
who is sensitive and sincere.

Moving Out of Dream Castles

My heart leaps when I feel his presence with me.
My spirit soars when we talk with each other.
I get excited anticipating what you have for our future.
Lord, why am I so attracted to him?

I need you Lord.
Help me to stay within your boundaries
so that I don't distort the picture.
I want to serve You and not my own lust.
You are the foundation of my life.
If I should pull that foundation out,
surely I will fail.

You are my source of life.
Without You I am nothing.
You are my strength and light.
If I move into darkness,
I shall stumble and fall.
I love you Lord and thank you
for trusting me with this union.

Now Lord, I give it back to You to control and mold.
I'm yours Lord, use me for Your purpose in this union.

Chapter 3 - Manifestation

Reaching the Impossible

As I think back to that moment,
my mind did not perceive the words
that came from your mouth.
All I received went straight
to my heart.

A scarce few words
can I even remember.
I only know what I felt.
It was comfort, affection and love.
It was peace, security and faith.

You reached out for me
when I didn't believe
it was possible for me to accept.
And I accepted
what I thought was impossible.

You see, I believed that
only God could touch me
expecting nothing in return.
But He used you to show me that
He put His love in a man who
could bring Him glory in a
simple expression of
unselfish love.

Thank you

Subliminal Messages

It was very subtle – quiet nudging
that can go unnoticed
if you're not aware.

It was a tender touch – soft caress
that seems insignificant
unless you're sensitive.

It was a soft answer – brief statements
that seem meaningless
if you're not listening.

It was a hand extended – reaching
that seems so small
unless you grasp it.

It was an ear listening – silence
that seems dormant
until you need to talk.

It was a good meal – nourishing
that satisfies only the stomach
unless you're hungry.

Chapter 3 - Manifestation

But, I was listening.

> I heard those subtle remarks.
> In grasping, I held on.
> I spoke in the silence.
> My hunger was satisfied.
> I'm sensitive to your touch.

I have come to understand your love for me.

Just a lookin'

"A good man?" I say –
while looking around.
But, I can't see him.

Looking for a good man?
Why?
I believe there are
plenty of good men.
I just don't know
what to look for.

Lord – open my eyes
so I can see the good man
you've got for me.
Suddenly,
God revealed him to me.
He's kind, considerate,
thoughtful and real.
I'm safe in his arms
with the warmth of his charm.
I know my heart he won't steal.

A gentleman at all times
and a friend to the end.
The simple things of life
are what we partake in.

He's humble, patient, meek and wise
yet strong, bold, proud and fine.

Chapter 3 - Manifestation

He was the nice guy in the grocery store
that I overlooked.
Though he held the door open
as I went through,
I never turned to say "Thanks"
cause I was off to the races.

At the coin laundry –
See right over there.
He's the one folding clothes
without a care.

I know a good man.
It's easy to see
the good man right here
looking at me.

Know This

I hope you know,
it's not my desire
to tie you down.
It's much more fun
seeing you completely free.

I hope you know,
it's not my desire
to change you.
I think it's more fun
watching you being yourself.

I hope you know,
it's not my desire
to entrap you.
It's more fun knowing
you want to be with me.

I hope you know,
it's not my desire
to dominate your time.
I know we have eternity.

I hope you know,
it's not my desire
to rush to places
you're not ready to go to.
It's more satisfying
when we walk in agreement.

Chapter 3 - Manifestation

I hope you know,
it's not my desire
to smother you with my affections.
It's more fulfilling
when we have room to breathe.

I hope you know,
it's not my desire
to rearrange your schedule.
I'm pleased just knowing you
set aside time for me.

I hope you know,
it's not my desire
to possess you.
I only want what
you offer me freely.

Unevenly Yoked

Darling,

There are kisses on my lips just for you. All you have to do is come and get them. Yet, I give up that privilege to tell you God's love is greater and his gift is eternity. You see, kisses can only last till the day of physical death.

My arms have waited so long just to hold you. Yet, that is nothing to me if I will not be able to meet you in eternity rejoicing before God forever.

God did not create us to eat, drink, be merry and die. He created us to have the most abundant life with Him on earth and at the death of the body continue with Him in spirit throughout eternity.

Chapter 3 - Manifestation

Understanding

I want to understand the true essence of your needs and know how to contribute to their fulfillment.

I want to see your dreams so that I may walk with you.

I want to anticipate your wishes so I know how to present myself to you.

I want to understand your thoughts as you express them to me.

I want to know your emotions by looking into your eyes.

I want to know you.

Voices From the Soul

Do you know I can feel your pain
and I want to comfort you?

I can feel your discontentment.
I try to find the words
but, they just won't come out.

I can feel your strain.
I wish I knew what to do.
You're sitting there upright.
Yet, I see it's not quite right.

Your words are noble – strong
with wisdom that rings its song.
Yet while you speak from the head,
I can hear the words of your heart.

Do you know I can feel your rain?

Whether or not you share what's inside,
it echoes a cry to my soul.
Whether or not you choose to reveal it,
I look through as an open window.

So, unfold for me what's locked in your heart.
It's too heavy for you alone.
Speaking with the Spirit of God
I have words to encourage your soul.

Chapter 3 - Manifestation

I assure you, you're not alone.
I tell you, I stand on your side.
To let you know I understand
To say God can tear down the walls

Do you know I can feel your pain
even though you try to camouflage?
You shield it with nobility.
You cover it with grace.
You hide it from the naked eye
but, I can see it on your face.

Your voice holds it's sound.
Your tone gives it away.
The moment I hear you speak
your soul calls my name.

It cries with sounds of joy.
It cries when there's a void.
It sings to me a musical melody.
It rings out the songs of your soul.

I wonder if you hear the voice of my soul.
I hope the message rings the comfort I behold.
I hope it speaks out loud, the desire to console.
I wonder if you feel the love inside of me.
I wonder if you feel the joy that fills my soul.

I pray you hear the voices
from my spirit and
my soul.

Gentle Tiger

I know you have the strength
and power
to rip me apart with one blow.
But you wouldn't harm me.
You're a gentle tiger.

I know you have the guile
and cunning
to creep behind me totally unaware.
Yet you wouldn't use that for a snare.
You're just a quiet tiger.

I know you have the wit
and charisma
to sweep me off my feet.
Though I'm sure you would keep me safe.
You're a noble tiger.

I know the roar of your voice
can make any heart flee.
Use it to ward off danger
and protect me.
You're a courageous tiger.

I know the world may cause
your anger to rage.
But you wouldn't strike you
at loved ones.
You're a temperate tiger.

Chapter 3 - Manifestation

I know you could pounce
leaving me totally helpless.
Only use your massive presence
to shield me.
You're a guardian tiger.

I know how powerful you are.
Your greatness is quite obvious.
No need to boast.
Retract your claws when you touch me
because you're a gentle tiger.

Hidden Treasures

You don't have that house you once described to me yet. You don't have that truck you want either. You don't feel your income is enough right now. Still my testimony is that you have treasures within you. What God has deposited in you can not be taken away.

You see, I realize that you are taller, bigger and stronger than me. Yet, you never exert strength to overpower me. You could easily overtake me but you always treat me like a precious treasure that you carefully hold on to. You hold me as a delicate vase that can easily be broken. You commit to the responsibility of my safety.

Even though God blesses you with wisdom, you don't try to force your ideas on me. It's OK that we disagree on some issues. You may even encourage me to see things a different way. But, it's done in a positive way. I appreciate that. I have come to believe you have my best interest at heart.

Don't take this the wrong way. I'm not trying to put you up on a pedestal. It is my desire to be a source of encouragement to you. I know you're not perfect. I'm sure you know what your short comings are. For the most part, people are quick to point them out. You know the pro's and the con's in your life. Rather than point out the negatives, I'd rather accentuate the positives.

Chapter 3 - Manifestation

People tend to think it takes grand pomp and circumstances to make a difference. I say, "It don't take all that." The simple consistent things you do are treasures in my heart I hold on to. As I'm driving along, I think about them and smile.

First Kiss

I was ready to go home. He walked me to the car as always. We embraced. I opened the car door and put my stuff in. As I was doing that, I could hear this faint mumbling behind me. Curious, I thought. It was kind of funny, but I didn't want to make a big deal out of it. So, I turned to say a final Goodbye. As I did, I could see these big boyish eyes looking at me. The excited face moved quickly and kissed me on the lips. I was shocked and delighted, yet my motions continued. I turned and flopped down in the car dropping the car keys that were in my hand. I don't know who looked the silliest, him or me.

Chapter Four

Appreciation

Now unto Him that is able to do exceedingly abundantly above all that we ask or think, according to the power that worketh in us. (KJV) Ephesians 3:20

Forgetting the Past

Thank you Lord,

I Thank You for letting me know how I'm going to get through the phase of lusting and sensuality in this relationship and in this cycle of my life. I stand on your word in Philippians 3:13-14 (NLT):

No, dear brothers and sisters, I have not achieved it but I focus on this one thing: Forgetting the past and looking forward to what lies ahead, I press on to reach the end of the race and receive the heavenly prize for which God, through Christ Jesus, is calling us.

I will forget all those past relationships I had in which I allowed lust and my very sensual nature to control me. They are dead relationships and are no longer a part of me. I am reaching for the promises of God before me now. The promise of the husband my Heavenly Father already selected for me.

I will not settle for less than the most explosive sexual relationship I could ever experience with my husband. I will not settle for sex that is not an absolutely free expression for me. I will not settle for ecstasy followed by tears of dissatisfaction because I broke a promise to myself and You by sinning against You and my own body. I will press toward the mark for the prize of the high calling (the marriage ordained by God – a holy matrimony).

Chapter 4 - Appreciation

I am looking forward to a bed undefiled. I am looking for uninhibited, unrestrained, free, pleasurable and fulfilling sex with my husband in marriage. I can no longer settle for sex tainted with guilt, shame and doubt. It restrains the best that I have to give. Anything less is a waste of time for me and my sex partner. I don't accept it. I will love my brother – my friend. I will not discredit him by trying to give him an imitation, knowing I can only give myself totally in marriage. By the power of the Holy Spirit, I accept no less, no way, no how. I give You permission to take control.

In Jesus' name.
AMEN

Lifetime Friend

Lord,

Right now, I'm satisfied knowing that I have a lifetime friend. I know that You will continue to enrich and mature our relationship as You have already designed. You know what lies ahead of us. You hold us in Your hand.

Thank You.

Chapter 4 - Appreciation

R-E-S-P-E-C-T

Knowing you is a blessing to me. I'm so proud to call you my friend. I've grown at least two inches since we met. Although, I tried expressing my gratitude as the weeks and months passed, I could never truly tell you exactly how I feel. You've always treated me with the utmost dignity and respect. A perfect gentleman as you promised. You always consider my feelings over yours. You never complain.

You will never know how much it means to me that you respect my values and standards. I have been ridiculed so many times when standing on God's principles of no pre-marital sex.

I heard:

"I don't believe you."
"I know you want me."
"You'll give in sooner or later."
"You have children. You didn't get them by yourself."
"You must have a man somewhere."

For a long time, those lines lured me into pre-marital sex because I didn't believe I could change. Finally, I decided to stand on my conviction, even if I stand alone. And it seemed like I was the only one. After a while, I began to believe in myself and God gave me His word to stand on.

This is my understanding of I Corinthians 6:18:

> Run from fornication. Every other sin man commits is outside of the body. But, when a man commits fornication, he sins against his own body.

I choose not to sin against my own body. Consequently, if I care about you, it's hard for me to watch you sin against your own body. It's not that I don't have a desire for sex because I do. But, with the help of the Holy Spirit, I don't fulfill that desire now. I love God more than my desire for sex outside of His will.

Thank you. I heard no sarcastic remarks from you. I heard no lines, no pressure and no jokes. Even though the desire was there, you didn't push it. Thanks again. I only heard your vote of confidence. I only see your respect. That means more than gold to me. You'll never really know how much you mean to me.

Chapter 4 - Appreciation

Hello Sunshine

While I am the dawn (Ladawn), you are sunshine – the complete manifestation of the dawn. In the dawn, you get a glimpse of the sun before it is fully risen. The dawn is a magnificent sight in itself. Yet it is only an introduction to the spectacular sunrise. In the sunshine all is clear and brilliant unless, of course, it is blocked by fog or storm clouds. Only faith allows us to know that sunshine remains above the rain. You are like sunshine to me.

I have a saying derived from Ephesians 3:20:

> God is able to do exceedingly abundantly above all that I could ever ask or even imagine.

I am experiencing that right now in our relationship. You are more than I ever imagined. My experience with you has been excellent. I'm just overwhelmed. I don't know if you realize how God has used you to impact my life. I am flattered that you think of me as an angel. In one respect I am as a messenger from God. Yet, in Christ, I am that and more. The angels are amazed that I am able to serve God by my choice and desire. Angels serve God by command.

Moving Out of Dream Castles

In past relationships I held on too tight, expected too much and made unrealistic demands. I learned a valuable lesson. I can't possibly hold on to someone who doesn't belong to me. Ultimately, you belong to God. So, I had to say, "Lord, help me to understand Your will for his life with all spiritual understanding." I had to say, "Not my will, Father. May Your will be done." I asked God to remove all of my intentions and ulterior motives for His. I wrestled with that idea for a long time.

Sometimes, I want to be your comforter. I must remember to acknowledge that God must be your true comforter. God loves you. Anything that I could give you in and of myself would only be temporary. Only what comes through me from God is lasting. I realize that God wants you closer to Him than you could ever be with me. You know, I enjoy time just for you. But the time I spend alone with God is extraordinary. I pray that you know that same experience.

Because our relationship is so important to me, I want to be able to submit mind, body and soul completely to the Holy Spirit within. I'm tired of bad relationships and my self-destructive way. I say I want to do things right, but I really want to do things my way.

Chapter 4 - Appreciation

I know the presence of God's spirit in me. I also know that I never completely surrendered. I have no self-control by myself. Day by day, I'm trusting God to guide me in the best way. I'm drawing closer and closer to Him. It would be injustice to draw closer to each other without drawing closer to God.

One thing obvious to me is that you possess the fruits of the spirit.

Love – Joy – Peace – Patience – Gentleness – Goodness – Faith – Humility – Self-Control

So, I am challenged to also "walk worthy of my calling in Jesus Christ."

Pray with me. Pray for the vision. If we catch the vision, we can stay on the path.

Love you

No Turning Back

Last month, I wrote a note about you in my journal:

> I could walk away from him with no guilt, no shame and no regrets.
> We have shared so much and I have truly been blessed.

Looking back today, I wish to erase that first statement. Walking away from you would be full of guilt, shame and regret.

Guilt would come just thinking I walked away from a brother and friend.

Shame because I walked away from a blessing instead of continuing to walk with you so that God may use me to bless you.

Regret because walking away from you is foolish when I know I really want to be included in your life.

Chapter 4 - Appreciation

Romance Without Sex

Lord,

I used to think it was ridiculous to even ask, "Can I have romance without sex?" Yet, you have shown me that it is possible and given it to me in this relationship. I'm getting more and more relaxed in his company. His voice is soothing to me. His shoulder is comforting to lay my head on. His word of understanding encourages me. His acceptance of me builds confidence in our relationship.

So, I'll ask another question. Can we have warm cuddly affection without submitting to sexual passion? Can we keep lust in control? Thank you for romance without sex. Is it possible to have affection without sex? Can I feel comfortable enough to cuddle in his arms without thinking about arousing him sexually or me for that matter? You have blessed me so richly.
AMEN

Desires

Thank you Lord,

I have come to realize it's OK to express my wants to you. I am able to turn them over to you. Then, You let me know if they are in line with Your desires for me.

Chapter 4 - Appreciation

Behind the Scenes

The play was fantastic. The stage setting and transition from one scene to the next was smooth. The integration of four different stories into one concise play was ingenious. The songs, prayers and praise were powerfully anointed. The message – well – I still meditate and absorb it. The actors were outstanding in every way. I replay each scene in my mind trying to capture the essence of it while the memory is fresh.

Witnessing the play and taking in the Word is like receiving fine diamonds or pearls. These are the jewels of life. Still, nothing impressed me more than having your company for the evening. You treated me like a Queen. Your very attentive gestures are priceless to me. I felt like nothing could harm me because you were my shield. First of all, you selected the best seats in the house. We were separated from the crowd with what seemed to be space of our own.

Second, I realize you made a sacrifice to buy those tickets. Thank you. I didn't have to concern myself with the cost. Being a single parent, head of the house and an accountant at work, I am always concerned with the cost of things. This one night, I did not have to even care. To this day, I don't know the price of those tickets. I didn't even try to find out. As a matter of fact, I didn't even see the tickets. I knew they were in your hands. That's all I needed to know.

Thirdly, from the moment we got into the car until the moment you took me back home, you ministered to me through your actions. Your actions spoke love to me. Once we got out of the car, you escorted me as a gentleman the entire evening. As we walked, the grass was not a place for our feet to cross. Your arm was a secure place to rest mine. On your side, we stepped parallel in pace. When guiding me down the stairs inside the theater, you held my hand and attended to my every step for safety. A lady has no fear following a man who knows the way.

Finally, God gave me beauty and the perfect attire. But, being with you illuminates the beauty in me. You took your awesome light and shined it on me by allowing me to be center of your attention rather than yourself. Thank you for acknowledging my internal and external beauty. Oftentimes, it's overlooked.

Today, I acknowledge your honor, your grace, your charm, and your nobility. You are a King among men with the humility of a shepherd. I acknowledge your strength. Strength is displayed when the stronger one seeks to protect rather than destroy. I acknowledge your integrity. Integrity is displayed when the wise one does not exploit the ignorant. Honor is having a standard and living by that standard no matter what state you find yourself in.

Chapter 4 - Appreciation

Your grace and charm speak for themselves. You always have decent conversation and a pleasant attitude. You never speak a degrading or even a discouraging word to me. All these qualities and more compile to form your nobility. It is this nobility that causes me to want to cling to you. This nobility encourages me to want more self-improvement.

I Thank God for building and shaping a man like you. I also Thank Him for allowing us to share this space in time.

Chivalry is not dead. It lives in you.

Love you

Counting My Blessing

Thank you for being patient with me.
Thank you for being a gentleman at all times just as you promised.
Thank you for honoring me as a lady.
Thanks for being a friend.

Thank you for being sensitive to my wishes, my needs, my moments.
Thank you for always extending your hand to help me up.
Thank you for walks in the park.
Talking in the fresh air always clears my head.
Thank you for holding me close as we walk.
Thank you for seeing through the invisible walls I have up
and trying to bring them down even if brick by brick.
Thank you for being a part of realizing a few of my dreams.
Thank you for sharing time with me that's not all complicated.
Thank you for being kind and gentle.
Thanks for caring, too.

Chapter 4 - Appreciation

Thank you for trying to build me up rather than tear me down.
Thank you for little kisses. Thank you for warm hugs.
Thank you for all the prayers I know you've prayed for me.
Thank you for overlooking all the mistakes I've made.
Thank you for forgiving me when I was just wrong.
Thanks for accepting me just the way I am.

I have a treasure of memories just of you.
I Thank God for every moment spent with you.
I just want to Thank you for just being you.
I hope I've been a blessing some way, somewhere, some how.
I hope some of my actions reciprocate my care.
Your efforts don't go unnoticed by me.
I wanted to let you know that.
Thanks again and again.

I could fill this page with Thank yous.
You've given me so much.

Intimate Friends

Lord,

It was one month ago that I asked if I could have affection without sex. I'm so amazed by Your revelations. I see it happening now. Thank you for allowing me to express my secret thoughts with him – things I had been keeping to myself. Thank you for allowing us to have an intimate friendship. There is so much fun, affection and conversation all rolled up in one.

I have:

A brother in Christ
A friend
A confidant
Someone I can trust
His respect
His care
His love

What more could I ask? Show me what I can do to make this relationship more meaningful to him. I ask You to continue blessing him. Meet him where he is. Touch him in a miraculous way that completely changes his life. I pray that he totally gives his life over to You. That's all he has to give You anyway. I don't want to take this privilege for granted.

Chapter 4 - Appreciation

Teach me how to interact with him in a way that honors You first then him. How do I reciprocate the honor that he has given to me? Make me aware of anything I do that dishonors, discredits or degrades him. Show me how to honor, encourage, inspire and uplift him. Once again, draw him even closer to You. Manifest Yourself to him so that he has a divine revelation of who he is in Christ and who You are in him.

Thank you again for the ability to have an intimate friend without having sex. Thank you for keeping me from fornication. You have been so gracious to give me what I want simply by my asking. I love you Lord and I'm depending on You to carry us on.

Bubbles

There are joy bubbles forming
deep down in my soul.
Little bubbles rising up
as visions unfold.
Look, you can see them.
There's one, then another,
And "OH" there's another.
Floating in my belly – then
Gently they pop, pop, pop-pop
popopopopopopopopopopopop
popopopopopopopopopopopop

There are joy bubbles flowing
as they multiply.
There's a fizzle in my spirit
as they glorify.
Hear them fizzle, fizzle
fizzzzzzzzzzzz
Streams of suds flow freely.
Joy bubbles overflowing
produce a twinkle in my eye,
releasing laughter in the sky.

Chapter 4 - Appreciation

Fortune Cookie

I was challenged when the waiter brought out the fortune cookies.
"I'll bet my fortune is better than yours."
"No," I refuted, "I'll bet my fortune is better than yours."
He took the two cookies in his hands before I could get one.
Next was the hand shuffle game.
"Close your eyes and pick one."
Although I thought it was unfair, I did.

As we were almost ready to leave the restaurant, we opened them.
I opened mine and smiled.
He opened his and smiled.
"I'll tell you what," he said "you read mine and I'll read yours."
We exchanged. As I read his, I realized that we had the exact message.
We must have realized it at the same time.
The message read as follows:

> Your love life will be happy and harmonious.

Well, I had to have the final word.
 "Still, mine is better than yours."
He wanted to know how that could be possible.
I answered, "Well, I read mine first."

Mesmerized

I hear the world in your voice
As you speak you give me your world.
Thank God for Jesus, we have eternity.
The stars will witness our immortality.
If the moon fades we march on forever.
The sun will shine till we no longer need its warmth.
The sound of birds reminds me of your love.

The Holy Spirit is our source and restoration.
By His power our love evolves daily.
Everyday it shines.
Everyday it sparkles.
Everyday we are special
and not just for show.
I'm astonished by your voice
and mesmerized by your touch.

Chapter Five

Reflection

But blessed are those who trust in the Lord and have made the Lord their hope and confidence. They are like trees planted along a riverbank, with roots that reach deep into the water. Such trees are not bothered by the heat or worried by long months of drought. Their leaves stay green, and they never stop producing fruit.
Jeremiah 17:7-8 (NLT)

Absence Makes the Heart Grow Fonder

It was almost a year ago. I made a decision about our relationship. I thought we would always be friends. But, let some time pass and some distance come between us. Then the infatuation would fade away. Maybe the over exhilaration would pass. Maybe the excitement I experience every time I hear your voice on the phone would change. Maybe I wouldn't continue to get lost in thoughts of you as I sometimes do. Maybe my intense emotions for you would moderate.

But it hasn't. I'm still infatuated with you. My whole demeanor changes when I hear your voice. I still find myself wishing for you at times when I feel all alone in this world. Sometimes, I am still obsessed with thoughts of you. And yes, you still have a tendency to appear in my dreams for time to time.

You are a very unique individual. There is something in you that fits perfectly with me. There is something about you that touches me in a way no one else can. I don't have words to express it, but I believe you know what I mean. I believe you feel it just the same.

Chapter 5 - Reflection

Gratitude

I told him to go home, but he wouldn't. He said that it seemed as if I summoned him. His friends were dumb-founded when he decided to leave the club to come see me. "All these beautiful women here and you want to leave?" They tried to talk him out of it to no avail.

So there he was at my door, "Did you summon me?" He was drunk and he came into the house with blessing abounding and praising God for these blessings. He went on to say, "Being with me brought him joy and peace." I could see the lust in his eyes and I was constantly watching his hands. Yet, behind all of that, there was a sincere message that he wanted to deliver.

It became real to me when he said, "Thank you for being a part of my life." Then he knelt down before me and continued:

"You taught me how to live. You showed me compassion and kindness when I was down. You gave me respect, dependability and integrity. You are part of me. What you added made my life better. God blessed me with a truck and money in my pocket. Soon, I'll be living in a much better place. Is there anything I can do to help you?

He insisted that he couldn't wait another minute to come tell me what was in his heart. Finally, he stood up and hugged me reciting this prayer.

"God bless this house. Bless everything around her. Bless her children and her children's children. Bless her with good blessings and if I have any extra blessings, give them to her."

He talked on and on about how I touched his life. The things he gained from me – money could not buy. He wanted to let me know that these were words that he couldn't keep any longer.

With tears streaming down my face, I was overwhelmed. Finally, he kissed my forehead and two cheeks. Then he left again just as he had come.

To God Be The Glory!!

Chapter 5 - Reflection

Marriage Bed Undefiled

Father,

I pray for the day when I can make love with the lights on and the bedroom door open. The room is at a good temperature so no bedspread is needed. With eyes open and a clear conscience, fully aware of what we're doing, I am with my husband in bed. I have no shame and nothing to hide. I want to scream to the top my lungs and feel good about it.

I want to know how to please my husband sexually and I want him to be pleasing to me. I want passionate uninhibited expressions that reach deep into the soul. I want to touch every part of him – head to toe. And when I finish, I want him to do the same for me. Then I want us to entwine together forming that bond as one. This is my desire.

I trust you to give me the best – what's perfect for me. I believe this is in line with Your will. I Thank You right now and I trust You for the manifestation.

Your loving daughter,

Ladawn

Dear Reader,

Thank you for your interest in **Moving Out of Dream Castles**. I pray God's blessing in your life. My home is in Atlanta, Georgia. E-mail me at ladawn_3@yahoo.com if you would like to bring the Dream Castles Poetry Hour to your ministry or organization. It's an hour of poetry and more. Together, we can discuss the poems and address questions like:

Am I only dreaming?
Am I deceiving myself?
Who's responsible for fulfilling my dream?
Who are the friends and users in my life?
Am I prepared to move out of the Dream Castle?
Do I know how to love?
Can I trust God for self-control?

The primary purpose for Dream Castles Poetry Hour is to examine the issues in the light of God's word.

Send me an e-mail. I'd love to spend some time with you or just hear your testimonies.

With humble regards,

Ladawn

www.ingramcontent.com/pod-product-compliance
Lightning Source LLC
LaVergne TN
LVHW021404080426
835508LV00020B/2450